T0414087

CAREERS *in Your Community*™

CAREERS *in* SOCIAL JUSTICE

Jessica Shaw

Rosen
YA
New York

Published in 2019 by The Rosen Publishing Group, Inc.
29 East 21st Street, New York, NY 10010

Copyright © 2019 by The Rosen Publishing Group, Inc.

First Edition

Library of Congress Cataloging-in-Publication Data

Names: Shaw, Jessica, 1972– author.
Title: Careers in social justice / Jessica Shaw.
Description: New York : Rosen Publishing, 2019 | Series: Careers in your community | Audience: Grade 7–12. | Includes bibliographical references and index.
Identifiers: LCCN 2018010328| ISBN 9781499467291 (library bound) | ISBN 9781499467376 (pbk.)
Subjects: LCSH: Social justice—Juvenile literature. | Social service—Juvenile literature.
Classification: LCC HM671 .S43 2019 | DDC 303.3/72—dc23
LC record available at https://lccn.loc.gov/2018010328

Manufactured in the United States of America

Contents

Introduction

The concept of social justice—the belief that society should offer equal opportunities, services, and privileges for all people—dates back to the earliest civilizations. The pages of history feature countless stories of courageous individuals who took the road less traveled and worked for social justice, even when facing fierce opposition and potentially dire consequences. Those who fought, in one way or another, for fair treatment not only raised awareness about important issues of their time, they paved the way for others wanting to work for social justice in their communities.

In the 1830s, members of the abolitionist movement worked to end slavery. In the mid-1800s, Elizabeth Cady Stanton, Susan B. Anthony, and others started the women's suffrage movement to give women the right to vote. Beginning in the 1930s, workers organized the American labor movement. As a result, labor laws went into effect that guaranteed a minimum wage, overtime pay, and protections for child laborers. In the 1950s and 1960s, social activists such as Martin Luther King Jr., Rosa Parks, and John Lewis helped to end legalized racial segregation and discrimination in the United States. The environmental movement had its humble beginnings in the 1940s, but took a huge leap forward in the 1960s and 1970s, as the public became more aware of the need to protect the environment and the potentially deadly consequences of not doing so.

Throughout history, there have been brave individuals and groups of people who have had to take a stand to achieve social justice.

Throughout the years of numerous campaigns for social justice, many community heroes have emerged. One such hero was Lucas Benitez. He was born in Mexico and at age seventeen moved to Immokalee, Florida, where he worked in the tomato fields. Angered by the unfair treatment and working conditions, Benitez helped establish the Coalition of Immokalee Workers (CIW) in 1992 and fought to end exploitation of all agricultural workers in America. Under Benitez's leadership, CIW launched a Campaign for Fair Food in 2001. This campaign made consumers aware of unfair practices and prompted retail food chains and supermarkets to sign agreements that required growers to improve wages and working conditions.

Born and raised in North Dakota near the Fort Berthold Reservation, Kandi Mossett championed many important causes in her community. She earned a degree in natural resource and park management and then a master's degree in environmental science and policy. In 2007, she became the Tribal Campus Climate Challenge organizer for the Indigenous Environmental Network, working with dozens of tribal colleges on environmental projects. Mossett helped implement recycling programs, solar panel installations, and community gardens, as well as organizing student campaigns against fracking on Native American lands and shutting down a waste disposal pit in the Native American community of White Shield, North Dakota.

At the heart of all these stories were brave people, determined to make things right. This same spirit has inspired many social justice movements and, eventually, created a multitude of jobs working for social justice.

Volunteering is always a great way to help, but there are also many career options. Professionals such as community advocates, social workers, and program coordinators are at the heart of every thriving community. They spend their workdays helping people in need and ensuring assistance and opportunities are available, especially to those who might not be able to reach out and find the help they need on their own. There are also a growing number of social justice careers that involve protecting and preserving natural resources and helping to improve air and water quality. Jobs in social justice are vital to the health and well-being of all communities, as well as future generations that will inhabit them.

CHAPTER One

Community Advocates: Giving Voice to the Voiceless

A community advocate is someone who champions a social issue, belief, or idea and works on behalf of individuals or groups to achieve desired outcomes. Often, community advocates provide support to those who are living in poverty or have a limited education. There are a number of areas of specialization in advocacy. For those who want to make a difference in their community, giving voice to the voiceless as a community advocate may be an ideal career choice.

Education and Experience for Community Advocates

There are many types of jobs in community advocacy. While all community advocates share a passion for helping people, the education and training requirements for

Community advocates offer a helping hand to community members in need, assisting them in overcoming many types of obstacles so they can lead happier, more successful lives.

specific positions in advocacy vary widely. Advocacy jobs that do not necessarily require a college degree include housing advocate, health care advocate, public policy advocate, and community organizer. Other positions, such as child advocate, disability advocate, and legislative advocate, generally require at least a four-year college degree and, in some cases, certification or licensure.

Experience as a volunteer or even personal experience dealing with a social justice cause can be influential factors for those who pursue this field of work. For example, someone who has experienced homelessness or who has seen a friend or loved one go through it will have a keen awareness of the need for housing advocates. In addition, he or she will most likely have great insights into the specific challenges and roadblocks faced by the homeless population. The most important attributes for all types of community advocates are compassion, excellent communication skills, and a willingness to support, defend, and speak up for others.

Housing and Utility Advocates

Housing and utility advocates work to help people living in poverty take care of their basic housing needs. Without a stable home, it's difficult for many other basic needs to be met. For people without a home, even ordinary, daily tasks are difficult. Holding down a steady job, receiving mail, eating nutritious meals, getting kids to school on time, and paying utility bills are all challenges for those without stable housing.

Housing advocates step in to help individuals or families who are struggling to find or retain housing or pay utility bills. In a typical work day, they may be meeting with clients directly or making numerous phone calls, helping them find affordable housing, assisting them in developing a budget, setting up housing or utility payment plans on their behalf, mediating any conflicts with landlords, locating resources to help provide for their basic needs, and providing assistance during times of crisis, especially during cold months when there are additional utility costs to heat a home.

Students who spend time volunteering in soup kitchens have the opportunity to help others while also gaining valuable experience for a future career in community service.

Housing advocates support policies and laws that make life a little easier for those living in poverty. They must stay up to date on the latest statistics and issues affecting the poor and homeless. High school students interested in a future career as a housing and utility advocate may want to spend time volunteering for homeless shelters in their communities, assisting in donation drives, or working at local soup kitchens or food pantries. These are all great things to list on a résumé and excellent opportunities to gain real-life experience in the field.

BUILDING A BUSINESS THAT GIVES BACK

Some people donate warm clothing to the homeless. Others donate their time, mentoring or teaching a valuable skill. And then there are people like Veronika Scott, who find a way to do both.

While in college, Scott was challenged by a college professor to design something that would "fill a need" in the city of Detroit. Though she was an art student, Scott didn't choose an art project that would offer citizens something that was visually pleasing. She wanted to make more of an impact. She took a good look at life on the streets of Detroit and chose to design something to help the large homeless population. She created a warm, waterproof jacket called the EMPWR coat that could convert into both a knapsack and a sleeping bag. Scott's goal was to provide warmth and a feeling of pride to those in need. She had succeeded in filling a need, but Scott didn't stop there. She was inspired by a woman in a shelter who shouted, "We don't need coats. We need jobs." Soon after she graduated from college, Scott decided to launch a nonprofit company and employ homeless people to make her coats. They would gain valuable training and job skills that would help them get back on their feet. At the same time, with more employees, Scott was able to make and distribute significantly more coats. She named her nonprofit the Empowerment Plan. Her employees were recruited from homeless shelters and had to go through a rigorous interview process. Tens of thousands of free coats for the homeless have been manufactured and distributed in the United States and around the world since 2012 by Veronika Scott's Empowerment Plan.

Health Care Advocates

Health care advocates are typically employed by hospitals, rehabilitation centers or other medical facilities, nonprofit organizations, government agencies, or insurance companies. Some health care advocates are self-employed. Health care advocates often help patients who are elderly, who have a language barrier, or who simply find their situation overwhelming. There are two types of health care advocates: patient advocates and medical billing advocates.

Patient advocates help patients and their caregivers navigate medical care and treatment. Often, it can be difficult for patients to fully understand their diagnosis and the medical services available, especially during a time of medical crisis. Patient advocates help patients understand their treatment plans and options. They make sure the patient's wishes are understood and can be instrumental in communications between the patient, the medical staff, and family members. Patient advocates might spend their day at a hospital, making sure the patient gets seen by the correct doctor and that the treatment plans have been fully explained to the patient and are being followed. Patient advocates often research specific health conditions and also spend time with the family or caretakers of a patient, ensuring everyone understands the diagnosis, treatment plan, and follow-up care that will be required.

Medical billing advocates are experts on the health insurance system. Their role is to make sure a patient's claims are filed, processed, and paid correctly. Medical bills can be difficult to understand. An important part of a medical billing advocate's job is to help patients understand the specific charges on their bill. Patients also may require help filling out paperwork for their insurance claims or following up on claims after they have been filed. Medical billing advocates spend a great deal of their time talking to insurance companies, medical providers, and patients.

Requirements for health care advocates vary widely, depending on the employer. Some health care advocates hold a bachelor's or master's degree in health care administration while others have a two-year associate's degree, and some work as health care advocates without any secondary education. All health care advocates do need specialized knowledge of medical terminology and health conditions, whether from advanced coursework or experience in the field.

Public Policy Advocates

Making a difference often goes hand in hand with bringing about change. Public policy advocates work to further the interests of their organization, with the goal of generating positive changes in policies related to their cause. Public policy advocates are frequently employed by nonprofit organizations, private companies, or academic institutions.

Job duties of public policy advocates include monitoring policies and procedures; educating the public, human service employees, and lawmakers about changes needed; and developing and executing advocacy strategies. Organizing and teaching other employees, volunteers, and community members how to be vocal supporters of the cause is another important function for public policy advocates.

Nonprofit organizations founded to promote causes such as HIV education and prevention or a cure for Alzheimer's disease are just two examples of types of employers who would want to have a public policy advocate on staff. Many companies, organizations, and agencies hire public policy advocates, but of course not all of them are involved in the struggle for social justice. When researching public policy advocate jobs, the search can be narrowed to include only organizations involved in social justice causes. Those organizations are plentiful, and there are many job opportunities as a public policy advocate for those who want to shape public policy as it relates to social issues in the community.

Disability Advocates

In 1990, Congress passed the Americans with Disabilities Act (ADA). Prior to passage of the ADA, there was no comprehensive civil rights law that specifically addressed the needs of people with disabilities. The ADA prohibits discrimination in the workplace or in hiring practices and mandates that reasonable allowances and accommodations must be provided with regard to public services, public spaces, and telecommunications. Some

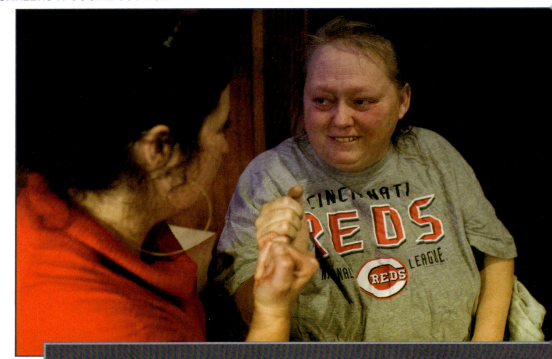

There are many people in desperate need who rely on disability advocates to help them with their Social Security disability claims.

people with disabilities are unable to work at all because of the nature of their disability. This makes it extremely difficult for them to financially support themselves or their families. In these cases, individuals who live in the United States can apply for Social Security disability benefits. The job of a disability advocate is to help people navigate the painstaking process of applying for Social Security disability benefits.

The vast majority of claims for Social Security disability benefits are initially denied. The Social Security Administration (SSA) has very strict criteria for applicants. In order to qualify, an applicant's disability must be on the SSA's approved list, and the applicant must prove that he or she is unable to work because of it. Disability advocates are specially trained to help qualified applicants get their Social Security disability claims approved. Many applicants seek out a disability advocate only after their initial claim is denied, but according to the SSA, everyone is entitled to representation by a disability advocate at any stage of the application or appeals process.

First and foremost, just as with all other types of advocates, disability advocates must have a passion for helping others. They must have a bachelor's degree and pass a certification exam on Social Security guidelines and disability regulations, and to maintain their professional certification as a disability advocate, they must fulfill continuing education requirements on an ongoing basis. Some disability advocates have earned a law degree and, as practicing attorneys, they specialize in disability advocacy. Disability advocates can expect to spend a great deal of time consulting with clients, reviewing statutes, staying current on any changes to disability rules and regulations, and even representing clients before an administrative law judge.

USING TECHNOLOGY TO IMPROVE LIVES

Three-dimensional (3-D) printers are specialized printers that can be programmed to create three-dimensional objects by applying repeated layers of material. This

(continued on the next page)

(continued from the previous page)

type of printer can create objects out of plastic or metal. There are many uses for this innovative technology, and one of them is using 3-D printers to create adaptive devices for people with special needs.

A group of high school students in New York took part in a very special 3-D project. They had visited pediatric patients at St. Mary's Hospital for Children, a facility that specializes in rehabilitative treatment for children with special needs. Many of the children needed specialized devices to assist them. The students were a part of Lynbrook High School's Advance Design and Innovation class, and they were inspired by their visits to the hospital. They decided to use their school's 3-D printer to build adaptive equipment for the children at St. Mary's. First, the students sketched designs and created prototypes. Next, they met with occupational therapists at the hospital to discuss how their designs could be improved. Finally, they began printing the devices, based on their finely tuned renderings. The devices they created included adaptive spoons, toys, wheelchair trays, and more. The students not only experienced the joy of helping children with special needs, they learned that a career in technology can go hand in hand with helping those in need to live life to its fullest.

Other Types of Advocates

Another job in community advocacy is that of victim advocate. Victim advocates are trained to help crime

As the official voice of many nonprofit and public interest groups, lobbyists play an important role in the fight for social justice and help to shape public policy.

victims, and some have a college degree in a related field. They may work in police stations, probation or parole offices, courts, or within nonprofit organizations such as domestic violence programs or crisis centers for victims of sexual assault. A typical day at work for a victim advocate might include providing a victim with emotional support, information on rights and options, referrals for supportive services, and help with safety planning. Victim advocates provide reassurance, comfort, and security to victims. Their role is vitally important in helping victims to come forward, tell their stories, and recover from their traumas.

Legislative advocates are also referred to as lobbyists. A college degree in political science or a related field and an in-depth understanding of the legislative process are essential for those interested in working as a legislative advocate. Their main objective is to directly influence legislation in accordance with the objectives of their organization. Their job duties typically include developing campaign strategies for their organization's cause, conducting research and producing reports, working to influence lawmakers, and training volunteers.

Another job in advocacy is that of community organizer. Community organizers unite people who live in the same community, inspiring, training, and leading them in achieving a common goal that they believe will improve the quality of life in their area. Community organizers recruit, interview, train, and schedule volunteer workers as well as planning events to raise awareness of their cause, creating marketing materials, and speaking at community events. They might work for political campaigns, organizations that advocate for victims, community action groups, crime prevention organizations, nonprofit organizations, or civil rights groups. Working as a community organizer does not typically require a degree, but excellent communication skills and effective leadership abilities are essential.

CHAPTER Two

Social Workers: Serving Those Most in Need

Social workers are mental health professionals who help individuals and families with many different types of issues, including relationship, health, and financial struggles. There are several areas of specialization within the field of social work, as well as a number of distinct work environments. Social workers are employed by hospitals, health clinics, schools, government agencies, and nonprofit organizations.

Education and Training Requirements

The fields of psychology and social work are closely related. Often, an initial interest in psychology leads students to a career in social work. Most high schools offer elective courses or dual credit courses in psychology and sociology. This is a great way to gauge interest and gain some basic knowledge about the field. Academic requirements for social workers include a postsecondary education. Social workers need a bachelor's degree in social work, and in order to increase potential income and job opportunities, most students

Medical social workers are especially important for patients who don't have a trusted family member available to support them as they recover from an illness or injury.

go on to complete two additional years of coursework for their master's degree. They must also pass the Association of Social Work Boards (ASWB) exam to obtain professional licensure. There are different levels of the exam, depending on where the student is in his or her coursework. Those who want to practice independently and diagnose and treat mental and behavioral issues must attain clinical certification as well. The requirements vary from state to state, but usually involve thousands of hours of supervised work experience and passage of a clinical licensing exam. Social workers are lifelines. They touch so many lives, young and old, and play a significant role in helping communities thrive. Social work is both challenging and rewarding and is a good fit for those who want to make a difference, one person at a time, each and every day.

Q&A WITH A SOCIAL WORKER

Emily Smith holds master of social work and master of school counseling degrees and is a licensed clinical social worker. She currently works for a large school district in Missouri. In the following interview with the author, she shares some great tips and insights for students considering a career in social work.

When did you know you wanted to be a social worker?

As a high school student, I knew that I had a passion for serving others and building lasting, organic, and meaningful relationships. During my senior year, I thought teaching was the path for me. Once I got to college and was able to explore various degree options, I discovered that social workers have an incredible ability to positively impact lives in a myriad of settings.

Do all social workers have a college degree?

Yes. Students who pursue a bachelor's in social work have a generalized degree and can work for a school, hospital, or nonprofit organization.

What are the advantages of earning a more advanced degree?

Students who earn their master's of social work (MSW) and those certified as licensed clinical social workers (LCSW) will find that there are a plethora of opportunities in their communities. They can also expect to earn somewhat more than those with only a bachelor's degree.

(continued on the next page)

(continued from the previous page)

What experiences might help prepare students for pursuing a career as a social worker?

There are a variety of opportunities high school students can pursue. The following opportunities involve working in an empathetic social setting and offer a glimpse of social work in action:

Volunteering for Habitat for Humanity
Volunteering at a nursing home
Volunteering in a homeless shelter
Helping out at a food pantry
Interning with or shadowing a social worker
Tutoring elementary students at low-income schools

Child, Family, and School Social Workers

Child, family, and school social workers serve many different functions in the community. They sometimes have the difficult task of removing children from unsafe homes and placing them in foster care. They may also take part in the rewarding experience of providing support and assistance to parents wanting to adopt. Where there is a financial need, they connect parents with resources to help them provide for their children. In school settings, social workers meet individually with students who are struggling, either with classmates or with some aspect of their home life. They also work closely with teachers and

Social workers talk to people about very personal issues and must be empathetic, trustworthy, and personable, as well as being knowledgeable and professional.

administrators on campaigns such as antibullying, mental health, test-taking strategies, and peer pressure. They may regularly meet with larger groups of students to discuss these and other issues. Social workers must provide a private, safe haven where children and families feel secure enough to talk about their struggles and divulge sensitive information, even when it may feel embarrassing or awkward to do so. They must also keep meticulous records. Often, a social worker's written account of observations or conversations with a child are used to substantiate claims of abuse or neglect so that the court system can step in to keep the child safe and healthy.

Medical and Public Health Social Workers

Medical or public health social workers need to have a great deal of knowledge about nutrition, health issues, and the health care system in addition to their qualifications as a social worker. Medical social workers are employed by hospitals, skilled nursing facilities, community health agencies, hospices, or outpatient clinics. Sometimes they are referred to as hospital social workers. They work with patients who are suffering from acute, chronic, or terminal illnesses. They offer emotional support and counseling to the patient and his or her family as well as help finding proper medical care and services. They can provide assistance with using important financial resources such as Medicaid and Medicare. Public health social workers are typically hired by government agencies or community health centers. They may focus on a particular health crisis in a community, such as obesity or diabetes, or they may offer a broad range of assistance. The goal of a public health social worker is to help communities stay healthy and thrive. Job duties might include setting up low-cost health clinics in the community, helping individuals find the health resources they need, educating the public about the benefits of proper nutrition, exercise, and healthy eating habits, or counseling community members about their specific health issues.

Mental Health Social Workers

Mental health social workers ensure individuals with mental illnesses get the care they need. Hospitals, mental

For some individuals suffering from mental illness, finding the help they need would not be possible without a mental health social worker.

health facilities, detention centers, rehabilitation centers, and community health centers employ mental health social workers. Mental health social workers often work closely with other mental health professionals such as psychologists, psychiatrists, therapists, and counselors. Their common goal is to stabilize the patient's mental health and provide the support needed for recovery. Many people who suffer from mental illness do not have the resources they need to treat their condition. Their loved ones are often unable to provide the support needed because they don't understand the condition. Mental health social workers are often their first recourse in trying to figure out how to deal with their mental illness. Initially, a mental health social worker will complete an assessment of the patient. If needed, they will counsel the patient about mental illness and available treatments. They may refer the client to a mental health professional such as a psychologist, depending on the severity of the condition. Mental illness can make it difficult to hold down a job and create great financial difficulty. Mental health social workers can help clients search for a job or apply for financial assistance, such as welfare benefits or disability benefits.

Forensic Social Workers

Forensic social work is also called criminal justice social work. It involves helping individuals who are in some way involved in the criminal justice system, including victims of abuse or neglect, incarcerated individuals, or recently released inmates. Forensic social workers typically have a strong clinical background so that they are qualified to complete psychological assessments, provide counseling, and initiate crisis interventions for individuals struggling to come to terms with recent trauma and associated challenges. They provide emotional support for those who have been victims of crime as well as those who have committed crimes. Forensic social workers help connect clients to resources such as housing assistance, mental health, and disability services. Those who work in a correctional facility offer their support to inmates during their incarceration as well as help assimilating back

Teaching life skills to incarcerated individuals is just one of many challenging and rewarding functions performed by forensic social workers.

into society upon their release. If inmates need special services such as mental health accommodations or suicide prevention services, a forensic social worker can identify and facilitate those needs. Forensic social workers who work with victims of crime will have completely different job duties. Their job is to provide therapy, legal guidance, and support to those who have suffered neglect or violence. They may lead interventions for those traumatized, serve as legal advocates, and create a bridge to essential resources. The emotional support and legal guidance provided by forensic social workers can make all the difference in the world for someone who has been a victim of a violent crime or emotional trauma.

CHAPTER Three

Environmental Crusaders

Beginning in the 1940s, an environmental movement began to take shape. There was a growing awareness of pollution and other factors that affect air and water quality. Eventually, awareness turned into

Beautiful green spaces for everyone to enjoy would cease to exist without the dedication and hard work of individuals who choose a career protecting and preserving the environment.

fear and outrage as knowledge about toxic chemicals in the environment increased. Over the next several decades, hundreds of human lives were lost and thousands of animals died in incident after incident involving the mishandling of chemicals and waste products. By the 1970s, the environmental movement had gained tremendous momentum. The first Earth Day was on April 22, 1970, with more than twenty million people across the country participating. It was an organized protest against environmental injustice and neglect and the largest demonstration ever in American history. The public outcry brought about a number of positive changes, but the struggle to protect the environment is not one that can ever end. There are many job opportunities for those interested in cleaning up the environment, preserving green spaces, or protecting animals and natural resources. Job responsibilities for those working in an office environment may include working on marketing materials, collaborating with other staff, educating community members, or working on budgetary issues. In the field, duties could include going door to door to gain momentum and funding for the cause, working directly at a site to improve conditions, holding public meetings and raising awareness, or training new employees or volunteers. At the highest level, engineers develop and test new technologies, scientists conduct environmental tests, ecologists study the relationship between an environment and its life-forms, and administrative staff make sure all employees are performing at the necessary level to meet or exceed goals.

Education and Training Requirements

A career in environmental justice is a good fit for anyone who feels strongly about working for meaningful environmental change and the development and enforcement of environmental laws that protect all people, in all communities, regardless of their income, race, color, religion, or national origin. The education and training requirements for these careers vary widely. There are entry-level positions in environmental justice that don't require any college coursework, such as a campaign staff member for a grassroots environmental movement, a special events assistant for an environmental group, or a fundraising representative for an environmental outreach campaign. In order to qualify for more advanced positions, a bachelor's degree in environmental science, environmental sociology, or a closely related major is advised. With a four-year degree, there are career options such as an environmental educator or any number of coordinator or management-level positions with organizations promoting clean energy, transportation, water, air, or green spaces. Experience outside of the classroom is also highly valued in this field. A master's degree in a more specific area is required for the highest-level positions.

Jobs Cleaning Up Communities

In 1948, Congress passed the Federal Water Pollution Control Act, the first legislation to protect water quality in the United States. That same year, twenty people died in Donora, Pennsylvania, and more than six hundred went

Before air quality legislation was passed, large cities often suffered from heavy smog levels because of fossil fuel emissions.

to the hospital when sulfur dioxide emissions descended in a dense fog over the area. It was one of many tragic events caused by pollution and a lack of regulation. Despite the incident in Pennsylvania, it wasn't until 1955 that Congress passed the Air Pollution Control Act. Over the next few decades, amendments were made to the air and water pollution legislation, and agencies such as the Environmental Protection Agency (EPA) were created to monitor and enforce the laws that protect the environment. The EPA is a government agency that employs a large number of people interested in a career devoted to a cleaner environment. There are entry-level positions within the EPA, such as environmental protection specialists or information technology specialists, and many other opportunities for those who have earned advanced degrees. There are also many grassroots organizations at work in communities around the world that are looking for employees to help them take up the fight for a cleaner environment.

In 1978, a reporter named Michael Brown had questions about a startling number of serious health problems and complications that had occurred from 1942 to 1952 in a community known as Love Canal near Niagara Falls, New York. An investigation revealed that a local chemical company had dumped more than 21,000 tons (19,051 metric tons) of toxic waste into the neighborhood canal. The toxic waste was found to be the cause of numerous birth defects, miscarriages, and abnormalities in children who lived there. The vast majority of environmentally hazardous areas, such as those areas around factories that produce dangerous byproducts, are located in marginalized communities where the property taxes and the potential for protests are low. Whether working for a large government entity like the EPA, or a smaller nonprofit organization devoted to making sure toxic waste is disposed of properly, there is a great need for watchdogs. People in communities such as Love Canal need an extra set of eyes. They need a voice. They need environmental crusaders on their side.

Another key component of protecting the environment is recycling materials. Every carton, can, jug, box, and jar that doesn't get recycled winds up in a public landfill. As more and more trash gets dumped in landfills, there is more concern about water runoff each time it rains. The runoff usually contains contaminants such as heavy metals and dangerous organic chemicals. Though most landfills have large storm water basins to collect the runoff, once they're full, the remaining water drains into the surrounding environment. Eventually, it finds its way into rivers and streams. There are also accidents that happen while waste is being transported to landfills. The US Department of Transportation reports that thousands of hazardous materials trucks are involved in accidents every year. Given the momentum and popularity of the environmental movement, it's no wonder that recycling efforts have multiplied so quickly since they first began in the 1970s.

Many businesses, schools, and private residences participate in local recycling programs. The growth of the recycling industry has opened up many new jobs, including jobs for drivers, sorters, machinery maintenance workers, facility managers, and sales representatives. These jobs are widely available to those who don't have a postsecondary education and are anticipated to be in increasing demand.

RYAN HICKMAN: RECYCLING ENTREPRENEUR

According to a 2013 report by the Environmental Protection Agency (EPA), Americans produced 254 million tons (230 million metric tons) of trash and 87 million of it was composted or recycled. This was a big leap from the rate of recycling in 1980, when only 15 million tons (13 million metric tons) of trash were recycled. Increasingly, people are realizing the importance of recycling. Even the youngest members of a community can make a big difference in recycling efforts. One such young man started helping his neighbors recycle even before he began kindergarten.

In 2012, Ryan Hickman was only three years old when he visited a recycling center in California and decided he wanted to play a role in recycling. His parents helped

(continued on the next page)

(continued from the previous page)

get the word out and he began collecting bottles and cans from neighbors. By the age of seven, Ryan had turned his passion for recycling plastic, aluminum, and glass into a business: Ryan's Recycling Company. Soon, Ryan had customers all across Orange County, California. In 2016, the story about Ryan and his company captured the attention of news organizations and talk show hosts. Since then, Ryan's story has been featured on dozens of radio and television programs. In his hometown of San Juan Capistrano, he was awarded "2017 Citizen of the Year." Most of the proceeds from Ryan's company go into his college savings fund, but sales of shirts with his company logo help support volunteer efforts at a local marine mammal center. Ryan's recycling efforts are a shining example of how anyone with a passion for making a difference can have a positive impact in their community while also earning money doing something they love.

Careers in Nature and Wildlife Conservation

Preserving green spaces and protecting endangered species are two important initiatives for those who believe everyone should be able to enjoy public land and the wildlife that inhabits it. Without the dedicated efforts of

Workers at wildlife refuges for endangered animals are committed to doing all they can to make sure beautiful creatures like this tiger are around for many years to come.

those working in conservation, eventually there would be no natural green spaces to enjoy, and many species would become extinct. Awareness of the importance of protecting wildlife and green spaces has steadily increased as awareness of air and water quality increased. Conservationists had been hard at work for decades before Congress passed the Endangered Species Act in 1973 to prevent the extinction of animals in the United States. Soon after, in 1975, the Eastern Wilderness Areas Act was passed to protect more than 200,000 acres (80,937 hectares) of national forest previously used for logging. There are a myriad of careers in conservation, whether students pursue work right out of high school or go on to earn an advanced degree. Some of the major organizations looking to fill nature and wildlife conservation jobs include: the Sierra Club, Audubon Society, World Wildlife Fund, Nature Conservancy, and National Park Foundation. Many cities have parks and recreation departments, and this can be a great entry point for students pursuing a career in conservation. Jobs such as campground manager, wildlife biologist, wildlife care specialist, park management and maintenance, or on the administrative and clerical side of organizations such as these are all possibilities. Some positions, such as a wildlife biologist, require a specialized degree, while others are available without completion of any post-secondary education. Many college students interested in conservation seek out entry-level jobs for a wildlife group or parks department while they are working on their degree.

THEODORE ROOSEVELT: THE CONSERVATIONIST PRESIDENT

Born in 1858, Theodore "Teddy" Roosevelt was known as a sportsman, hunter, and conservationist long before becoming president in 1901. He had seen firsthand the effects of things like overgrazing and pollution. At a time when most people still considered North America's natural resources inexhaustible, Roosevelt knew better.

After he became president, Roosevelt had the power to do something about his concerns for the environment. He wanted to ensure the sustainability of the country's resources and prevent the loss of animal species and their habitats. He wanted future generations of Americans to have the same natural resources and wildlife to enjoy. And, largely because of his actions, precious green space and national monuments are enjoyed by millions today. In order to conserve forests, Roosevelt created the United States Forest Service (USFS), an organization within the Department of Agriculture. Under his leadership, 150 national forests were established. He passed the National Monuments Act and declared eighteen sites as national monuments, including the Grand Canyon. His work didn't stop there. Roosevelt established five national parks, four national game preserves, and fifty-one federal bird reserves. All in all, Roosevelt protected 230 million acres (93 million ha) of public

(continued on the next page)

(continued from the previous page)

land during his presidency. His bird and national game preserves eventually became national wildlife refuges that are now managed by the US Fish and Wildlife Service. Roosevelt was a conservationist ahead of his time. His legacy is seen in the beauty of natural resources throughout the United States, and his efforts have inspired scores of conservationists who follow in his footsteps, working to protect green spaces and wildlife for all to enjoy.

Teddy Roosevelt poses for a photo at the Grand Canyon, one of many natural sites he wanted to preserve for future generations to enjoy.

Working for Clean Energy and Transportation

Jobs in clean energy and transportation, ranging from entry-level to advanced positions, can be found within nonprofit organizations and in both public and private sectors. Efforts to reduce the use of petroleum and find innovative ways to provide sustainable energy sources have created an increased demand for employees in this field for a wide variety of jobs. In 1993, the US Department of Energy began its Clean Cities program in an effort to cut petroleum use in transportation. Since then, more than 8.5 billion gallons (3 billion liters) of petroleum have been saved. The US Department of Energy offers jobs in many disciplines, including science and engineering and program analysis. Organizations like the Blue Planet, Sierra Club, Calstart, International Council on Clean Transportation, and major automobile manufacturers such as Tesla and General Motors have added thousands of jobs in clean energy, including in transportation and logistics, research and development, and the creation of electric batteries. More companies continue to get onboard with clean energy initiatives, making this a promising field for those looking for a challenging career that helps the environment.

CHAPTER Four

Program Coordinators

Program coordinators often work for universities, youth organizations, health care organizations, or any number of nonprofit organizations. Program coordinator positions usually require a college degree. Previous experience working or volunteering with populations similar to the program's customers is also preferred. For example, a youth program coordinator might have volunteered with youth at church or worked as a babysitter. A health care program coordinator might have volunteered in a nursing home. A nonprofit program coordinator quite possibly had previous volunteer experience with nonprofits. Strong leadership, organization, communication, and social skills are vital to success in all program coordinator positions.

Youth Program Coordinators

Youth program coordinators work for organizations such as the YMCA, Boys & Girls Clubs of America, Boy Scouts of America, and Girl Scouts of the USA, as well

Youth program coordinators are known for their energy, enthusiasm, friendliness, and ability to not only lead and engage in youth activities, but to have fun doing so!

as for church, housing assistance, and after-school programs. They hire and train staff, supervise activities, and plan and execute new recreational or sports activities for youth participants. Preparing reports, maintaining a professional relationship with customers and community partners, evaluating staff, and creating the schedule are also part of the job. Youth program coordinators are also needed to manage camp programs, where additional responsibilities would include supervising cabin activities, ordering supplies as needed, and inspecting recreation areas to ensure safety standards are being met. Additionally, in a camp setting, a youth program coordinator would live onsite and might be expected to complete training in a variety of activities, such as archery, ropes course, canoeing, fishing, and lifeguarding. These positions are often only seasonal, but if offered through an organization like the YMCA, there are also youth program coordinator positions available in their facilities, year-round. Successful youth program coordinators are young at heart. They enjoy engaging in fun activities with kids of all ages, not just supervising them. This type of position is a good fit for those who enjoy

Planning events for local youth groups such as fund-raisers, parades, and educational opportunities is an important function of program coordinators.

working with young people and making a difference in their communities.

Health Care Program Coordinators

As the name implies, health care program coordinators work in the health industry. They might find employment with nonprofits, public health agencies, hospitals, or assisted living facilities. A master's degree is often

A HISTORY OF SERVING YOUTH: YMCA

The very first YMCA was organized in London in 1844, with the first US YMCA organized in Boston in 1851. From its humble beginnings and small membership, the YMCA has grown to become a leading nonprofit organization for youth development. At the heart of the organization is their commitment to strengthening communities and helping to provide everyone, regardless of age, income, or background, with the opportunity to thrive. With thousands of locations across the United States and a multitude of youth and family programs, from summer camps to organized sports to volunteer opportunities, the YMCA is a leading employer of program coordinators who enjoy helping others achieve a healthier lifestyle.

required for this job. Candidates for a position as a health care program coordinator must have knowledge of health issues and health intervention for specific problems. Health care coordinators handle all facets of program administration. They are responsible for ensuring the specific treatment options offered at the health care facility—such as a smoking cessation program or tuberculosis screening—are successful. This includes supervising staff members, maintaining meticulous records, refining procedures, submitting reports, preparing budgets, and developing plans and goals. Developing and delivering health programs and treatments that promote the well-being of clients is the most important function of a health care program coordinator. Educating clients on health risks, conducting health screenings, and coordinating their access to benefits are examples of tasks a health care program coordinator does on a regular basis. In addition, advocating for legislation that would improve the health care system might also be required. Program coordinators frequently have to work with outside groups, whether to plan a program that will serve members of a particular group, or to coordinate efforts with partners such as community hospitals, the local health department, or drug treatment centers. Fundraising efforts, creation of educational pamphlets, and handling media relations are also common day-to-day tasks for health care program coordinators.

Education Program Coordinators

Program coordinators that work for universities are sometimes called education program coordinators. They

Some education coordinator positions involve overseeing adult education programs for those who have returned to school later in life or those who are nonnative speakers.

perform a variety of functions to help sustain an engaged, vibrant student population. For this position, there are sometimes opportunities for applicants with only a high school diploma if they also have experience related to the job responsibilities. An education program coordinator manages specific program activities, plans and implements programs, aids in the development of policies and procedures, and creates, publishes, and markets promotional and educational materials about the program. Frequent communication and interaction with students, staff, and other individuals involved in program activities is required, as well as budget planning and management of expenditures. An education program coordinator often plays a key role in a university's recruitment efforts, showcasing the programs and activities the school has to offer.

Nonprofit Program Coordinators

Employees of nonprofit organizations consistently report having a high degree of job satisfaction. In general, nonprofits are known for providing great benefits to their employees, often including perks such as tuition reimbursement, fitness facility memberships, flexible hours, and generous vacation time. The fact

Nonprofit organizations such as Habitat for Humanity operate in communities around the world and offer volunteer opportunities building homes and working in their stores.

that nonprofits are organizations devoted to making positive changes in the world is icing on the cake, giving employees the opportunity to enjoy a great work environment while also offering help and support to those who need it the most. Many types of program coordinators find employment with nonprofit organizations. Day-to-day job duties include scheduling, monitoring the budget, fund-raising, managing staff members, forming partnerships with community businesses and other organizations, and distributing marketing information. In a 2017 report by the careers site Indeed.com, some of the top nonprofits to work for included Habitat for Humanity, AARP, Salvation Army, Boy Scouts of America, Girl Scouts of the USA, YMCA, Boy and Girls Club of America, Easter Seals, and Communities in Schools. In a story published on the *Time* magazine website in September of 2017, Indeed's senior vice president Paul D'Arcy said, "Employees seem to be very satisfied and happy to work for a mission-driven organization that helps a community they are passionate about." Making a living while making a difference is a win-win for millions of nonprofit employees around the world.

CHAPTER Five

Landing a Rewarding Career

Choosing the right career path is a big decision. Many people are never fortunate enough to enjoy going to work each day. Making enough money to be financially stable is important, but finding a job that's challenging, emotionally rewarding, and meaningful on a personal level is equally important. For those who decide to pursue a career in social justice, there are skills, experiences, and resources that are essential when it comes time to land that perfect job.

Volunteer Experience

Volunteer experience is a great opportunity for personal growth, regardless of profession, but because social justice careers are often with organizations that work closely with volunteers and/or share the common goal of strengthening the community, volunteer work is especially important for students who hope to work in social justice.

Helping to build homes for those in need is just one example of a rewarding volunteer opportunity that will make an applicant's résumé stand out.

There are many personal and professional advantages gained by volunteering. Volunteer work hones job-related skills, such as teamwork and organization, and provides opportunities to network with community and business leaders. It's a chance to see, firsthand, what it might be like to work in a specific profession before deciding to commit to that field. Recent graduates sometimes struggle with not having any experience to list on their résumé. Volunteer work not only fills that hole in a résumé, it speaks to an applicant's character. Applicants who have given their time, selflessly, and shown a genuine interest in gaining knowledge and working for positive change stand out from those without volunteer experience. A résumé is an applicant's chance to make a strong first impression, even before sitting down for an interview. A report from the Corporation for National and Community Service states that volunteers are 27 percent more likely to find employment than nonvolunteers.

Aside from ensuring an applicant's résumé stands out from the crowd, volunteer experience also promotes a healthy lifestyle and sense of well-being. Research gathered by the University of Exeter Medical School found that volunteers enjoyed a number of health benefits, including lower rates of depression, greater ability to handle stress and recover from illness, and overall, a longer, happier lifespan. Volunteer opportunities are plentiful in every community. There is always a need for volunteers in hospitals, homeless shelters, animal shelters, schools, and with local hospice organizations. There are also a number of organizations such as Big Brothers Big Sisters who have a need for mentors who can spend quality time with a child, tutoring them, enjoying a recreational activity, and just talking with them. Many volunteer organizations require a background check and have a minimum age limit for their volunteers, but a number of them accept—and even seek out—teen volunteers. Those who participate in volunteer activities reap many health benefits, have a better chance of landing a job they will enjoy, and go to sleep each night knowing that they are contributing to their communities in a meaningful way.

The Job Search

Free, online resources for job seekers are abundant. There are so many, in fact, that deciding which sites to use can be overwhelming, especially for those new to the job search process. Some sites are more user friendly than others and have search tools that are easy to use. A 2017 web article on the Balance, a personal finance site, evaluated hundreds of job search sites and listed their top ten: Indeed, CareerBuilder, Dice, Glassdoor, Idealist, LinkedIn, Monster, US.jobs, Google for Jobs, and LinkUp. Using several job search sites is optimal, since not every employer lists available jobs on every job site. Other helpful resources include Facebook groups or sites, such as Hired or Simply Hired, that allow job seekers to post their specific requirements anonymously to avoid unwanted emails about jobs that don't fit their requirements. Attending a local career fair is another free option that gives job seekers the opportunity to talk with representatives from many different companies at one location. Some organizations actually conduct interviews during the career fair for those who wish to apply.

Job search sites such as LinkedIn have made it easy for job seekers to research available jobs, assess their skills and qualifications, and apply for jobs that are a match.

An online presence can be a powerful tool for networking and learning more about companies and organizations that are of interest when job searching. Social media platforms such as Facebook, Instagram, and Twitter are some of the most popular. Typically, users post personal pictures, comments, and information on these sites to engage and stay in touch with family and friends. It's important to remember, however, that family and friends are not the only people who might see those

BUILDING A REMARKABLE RÉSUMÉ

Hiring managers often have a mountain of résumés to sift through when choosing which candidates to call in for an interview. Each résumé has only a few seconds to make a first impression and land in either the "yes" or the "no" pile. There are a number of ways to help a résumé soar instead of sink and land that interview.

1. Double and triple check for typos, grammar, spelling, and formatting.

2. Use bullet points rather than complete sentences when highlighting strengths.

3. Customize résumés for each specific employer, based on what they are looking for in an employee.

4. Use action words and be clear, succinct, and specific in describing accomplishments.

5. Show enthusiasm and confidence without crossing the line into arrogance.

posts. Employers who are considering hiring an applicant will frequently look them up on the internet. Images, photos, and comments that are fine for family or friends to see might not necessarily reflect the qualities employers are looking for in a new hire. Utilizing privacy settings and limiting access is helpful, but the safest route is to carefully consider all content before posting.

The Interview Process

Interviews can be nerve-racking and intimidating, especially for those who are searching for their first job. Most people experience some amount of anxiety, but properly preparing for an interview can boost confidence and take the edge off. Watching mock interviews can be very helpful, and there are also several TED Talks on

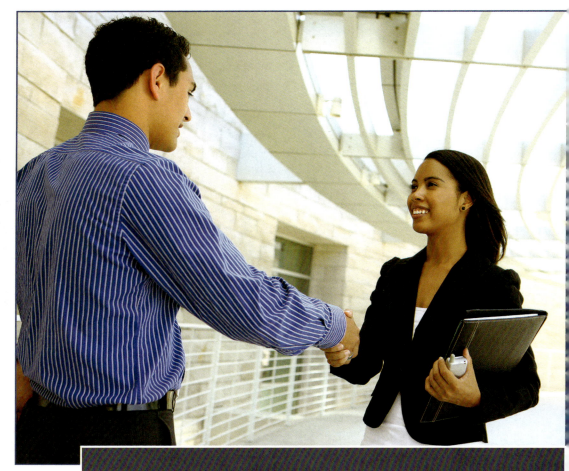

Making eye contact, displaying confidence, and being both friendly and professional will help make an excellent first impression when interviewing for a job.

interviewing. After watching mock interviews, applicants should think about questions they might be asked in an interview as well as questions they might ask of the employer during the interview. Choosing a friend, family member, or mentor and holding a practice interview is next. The practice interview should replicate a real interview as closely as possible, with the interviewee wearing business attire and staying in character the entire time, rather than joking with the hiring manager or getting tripped up by a question and saying, "Wait, let's start over." Practice interviews that are treated as real interviews, from start to finish, give the job seeker a true advantage when it's time for a real interview. At the end of the exercise, constructive feedback from the interviewer helps determine where the interviewee needs improvement. The more practice interviews, the better. Questions can be varied, and several different interviewers can be used to help the interviewee feel fully prepared. Lastly, before the interview, applicants should learn as much as possible about the company or organization.

Making a great first impression is important. Though appropriate interview attire varies, depending on the position being applied for and the type of company, looking neat and professional is the rule for any job interview. In general, jeans, sandals, sneakers, T-shirts, and excessive makeup or jewelry should be avoided. Clothes should be clean and unwrinkled, nails trimmed, and hair combed or styled nicely. Suits are always a good option, even if the job itself would not require wearing one. Professional attire and preparedness for the interview are major factors when hiring managers are deciding who gets the job.

Following up after an interview is a professional courtesy and a nice touch, as well as one more chance for applicants to get their names in front of prospective employers. This can be as simple as an email thanking

COMMON INTERVIEW QUESTIONS

Every applicant wants to put his or her best self forward during an interview. It can be difficult to feel strong and confident, though—especially for first-time interviewees. Some questions asked by the interviewer will be unique to the position or company, but others are fairly standard and can be anticipated in advance. Thinking about how best to respond to these common interview questions can go a long way toward feeling well prepared.

1. Why are you interested in this position?
2. Why do you feel you would be a good fit for this position?
3. What do you consider your greatest strengths?
4. What do you consider your weakest areas?
5. What do you know about our company/organization?
6. If hired, when are you available to start?
7. What are your long-term career goals?
8. Do you have any questions?

them for their time and consideration or a formal letter in which the applicant highlights relevant skills and strengths, mentions anything that may have been forgotten during the interview, and thanks the interviewer. Many applicants don't take the time to do this, so those who do will definitely stand out.

With such a wide variety of career options in the field of social justice, it makes sense that there is also a great deal of variation in salaries and job outlook. Though projections specific to each career within the field of social justice are not listed, the Bureau of Labor Statistics (BLS) predicts an increase of 109,700 social work jobs between 2016 and 2026. This represents a much faster than average rate of job increase, at 16 percent. Many community advocate positions are closely related to the Health Educators and Community Health Workers designation with the BLS. For those positions, the increase in number of jobs between 2016 and 2026 is expected to be 19,200, which will be a 16 percent increase. Conservation scientists and foresters help manage the land quality of forests, parks, and other natural resources. The BLS prediction for this field is that there will be a 6 percent increase in jobs between 2016 and 2026, which equates to 2,000 new jobs. Environmental engineers are specifically involved in efforts to reduce water and air pollution and improve recycling and waste disposal methods. The BLS projection is that they will see an 8 percent increase in job growth between 2016 and 2026, which will mean 4,500 new jobs. Program coordinator positions most closely align with the BLS category of social and community service managers. The number of jobs in this category is expected to have an 18 percent growth rate between 2016 and 2026, which

As long as there are social causes to fight for and work toward, there will continue to be job opportunities for those willing to take on a challenging, meaningful career.

would equate to 26,500 new jobs. All social justice careers represented in these BLS categories are expecting at least average job growth, with some projected to have much faster than average growth through 2026.

Job seekers who want to work in social justice will find numerous meaningful job opportunities. There are positions for high school graduates as well as for those with a college degree. In addition to a multitude of jobs projected to grow significantly at least through 2026, careers in social justice have other significant benefits to offer. Careers that involve advocacy, nonprofit work, and work that fosters positive changes that strengthen communities offer candidates a chance to feel great about what they do every day at work, what they are giving back to their communities, and the legacy they are leaving behind. Working in a job that helps to solve social problems and unite others in passionate defense of every citizen's basic rights and privileges means sleeping well at night, knowing that the workday is about more than just paying the bills.

Glossary

ABOLITIONIST A person who believed in putting an end to slavery.

ACTIVIST A person who works to bring about positive social or political change.

BYPRODUCT A product that's created unintentionally while manufacturing something else.

CLEAN ENERGY Energy that doesn't cause pollution, like coal and oil do.

COMPOSTING Combining leftover organic material such as scraps of food with leaves and yard waste, allowing it all to decompose, and then recycling the organic material as fertilizer.

CONTAMINANT A toxic substance that pollutes something.

DIRE A situation that is urgent and possibly disastrous or deadly.

EMISSIONS Substances such as gases or small particles released into the air that cause pollution.

EMPATHETIC Understanding of others' feelings.

ENTREPRENEUR Someone who starts his or her own business or company.

EXPLOITATION Benefitting from the use of resources without regard for the harmful effects.

GRASSROOTS An initial, basic level of an organization or campaign.

INCARCERATED Imprisoned and held captive after being found guilty of a crime.

INDIGENOUS Native to a particular place.

LANDFILL A site used for disposing of waste.

MEDICAID A government health care program that helps cover medical costs for low income individuals.

MEDICARE A federal health insurance program for individuals over the age of sixty-five.

MYRIAD A multitude or great number of.

PLETHORA An excess or great amount of something.

POSTSECONDARY EDUCATION An education beyond high school.

PROTOTYPE An initial model or design of something.

RECYCLING Finding a way to reuse waste material instead of throwing it away.

RUNOFF The water, soil, debris, and potential contaminants that drain away from an area of land where no more water can be absorbed.

SUFFRAGE The right to vote.

For More Information

Centre for Social Justice
720 Bathurst Street
Toronto, ON M5S 2R4
Canada
(416) 927-0777
Website: http://www.socialjustice.org
The Centre for Social Justice is an organization devoted to
    peace and security for everyone. Their website offers
    information on their research, education, and advocacy
    efforts to bring people from all faiths and income levels
    together in the pursuit of equality and democracy.

Charity Village
8170 Lawson Road
Milton, ON L9T 5C4
Canada
(800) 610-8134
Website: https://charityvillage.com/cms/about-us
Facebook, Twitter, and Instagram: @charityvillage
Charity Village is an excellent resource for information
    about and collaboration within Canada's nonprofit
    sector. The website offers online courses, job listings,
    and the latest nonprofit news.

Environmental Protection Agency (EPA)
1200 Pennsylvania Avenue NW
Washington, DC 20460
(202) 564-4700
Website: https://www.epa.gov
Facebook: @EPA
Twitter: @epa
Instagram: @epagov

The EPA is an organization committed to protecting human health and the environment. Their website provides information on careers, laws and regulations, and policy and guidance documents.

Food First
398 60th Street
Oakland, CA 94618
(510) 654-4400
Website: https://foodfirst.org
Facebook: @foodfirst
Twitter: @foodfirstorg
YouTube: FoodFirstVideo
The goal of the Food First organization is to work toward systemic change in the world that will end hunger. Their website provides the latest information and research on the global food supply, annual reports, and postings about political action events.

Idealist
302 5th Avenue, 11th Floor
New York, NY 10001
(212) 843-3973
Website: https://www.idealist.org
Facebook: @TheIDEAlistRevolution
Twitter: @idealist
Idealist is an organization whose mission is to connect people, organizations, and resources for the greater good. Their website lists opportunities for people who want to do good.

National Coalition for the Homeless
2201 P Street NW
Washington, DC 20037
(202) 462-4822
Website: http://www.nationalhomeless.org
Facebook: @NationalCoalitionfortheHomeless
Twitter: @Ntl_Homeless
The mission of the National Coalition for the Homeless is
    to protect the civil rights of the homeless population
    and work toward preventing and ending homelessness.
    Their website features information about homelessness,
    health care, employment, career opportunities, and
    social campaigns.

Sierra Club Foundation
2101 Webster Street, Suite 1250
Oakland, CA 94612
(415) 995-1780
Website: https://www.sierraclubfoundation.org
Facebook: @SierraClub
Twitter and Instagram: @sierraclub
The goal of the Sierra Club Foundation is to educate and
    encourage people to protect the natural environment.
    Their website includes information on the many
    environmental movements they are a part of.

For Further Reading

Conger, Cristen, and Caroline Ervin. *Unladylike: A Field Guide to Smashing the Patriarchy and Claiming Your Space*. New York, NY: Ten Speed Press, 2018.

Cox, Lisa E, Carolyn J. Tice, and Dennis D. Long. *Introduction to Social Work: An Advocacy-Based Profession* (Social Work in the New Century). Thousand Oaks, CA: Sage Publishing, 2018.

Creighton, Allan, and Paul Kivel. *Helping Teens Stop Violence, Build Community, and Stand for Justice*. Alameda, CA: Hunter House, 2011.

Harrigan-Pedersen, Nurys. *Make Your Mark: The Smart Nonprofit Professional's Guide to Career Mapping for Success*. New York, NY: Morgan James Publishing, 2018.

Jansson, Bruce S. *Becoming an Effective Policy Advocate: From Policy Practice to Social Justice*. 7th ed. Belmont, CA: Brooks/Cole, Cengage Learning, 2014.

Lowe, Ben. *Doing Good Without Giving Up: Sustaining Social Action in a World That's Hard to Change*. Downers Grove, IL: InterVarsity Press, 2014.

Miller, Mark M. *Economic Development for Everyone: Creating Jobs, Growing Businesses, and Building Resilience in Low-Income Communities*. New York, NY: Routledge, 2017.

Moye, J. Todd. *Ella Baker: Community Organizer of the Civil Rights Movement* (Library of African American Biography). Lanham, MD: Rowman & Littlefield Publishers, 2013.

Padgett, Deborah, Benjamin Henwood, and Sam Tsemberis. *Housing First: Ending Homelessness, Transforming Systems, and Changing Lives*. New York, NY: Oxford University Press, 2016.

Petrikowski, Nicki. *Working for Tolerance and Social*

Change Through Service Learning. New York, NY:
Rosen Publishing, 2015.

Sack, Rebekah. *The Young Adult's Survival Guide to Interviews: Finding the Job and Nailing the Interview.* Ocala, FL: Atlantic Publishing Group, 2016.

Torrey, Trisha. *So You Want to Be a Patient Advocate?: Choosing a Career in Health or Patient Advocacy.* Baldwinsville, NY: DiagKNOWsis Media, 2015.

Waite, Marilyn. *Sustainability at Work: Careers That Make a Difference.* New York, NY: Routledge, 2016.

Bibliography

Ayers, Mike. "What Are the Best Nonprofits to Work For? | Money." *Time*, September 26, 2017. http://time.com /money/4956200/these-are-the-15-best-nonprofits-to -work-for-and-they-have-thousands-of-open-jobs.

Calhoun, Marissa. "Coat Provides Warmth, Jobs to Detroit's Homeless." *CNN*, June 10, 2016. http://www .cnn.com/2016/03/10/us/cnn-heroes-veronika-scott -detroit-homeless/index.html.

Cherry, Kendra. "What Does It Take to Be a Social Worker?" Verywell Mind, August 4, 2017. http://www .verywellmind.com/what-is-a-social-worker-2795656.

Disabled World. "Assistive Technology: Devices, Products and Information." September 27, 2017. http://www .disabled-world.com/assistivedevices.

Dreier, Peter. "19 Activists Who Are Changing America." Huffington Post, October 28, 2013. http://www .huffingtonpost.com/peter-dreier/progressive -activists_b_4171399.html.

EnviroEducation.com. "Environmental Justice: Academic Requirements, Professional Outlook—EnviroEducation. com—Directory of Environmental Schools and List of Environmental Programs." February 2, 2018. http:// enviroeducation.com/resources/environmental -justice-academic-requirements-professional-outlook.

Huang, Georgene. "6 Overlooked Job Search Resources to Help You." *Forbes*, June 29, 2017. http://www .forbes.com/sites/georgenehuang/2017/06/27/6 -overlooked-job-search-resources-to-help -you/#6bea3be2e8e4.

Learn.org. "What Are the Job Duties of a Program Coordinator?" January 15, 2018. http://learn.org /articles/What_Are_the_Job_Duties_of_a_Program

_Coordinator.html.

Louie, Kaitlin. "Introductory Guide to Forensic Social Work (Criminal Justice Social Work)." 2U.com, January 20, 2018. http://www.onlinemswprograms.com/features /guide-to-forensic-social-work.html.

Lucas, Kenya. "Duties of a Health Care Program Coordinator." Chron.com, January 10, 2018. http:// work.chron.com/duties-health-care-program -coordinator-25994.html.

Mitchell, Maxine. "Lynbrook High School Students Present 3D Printed Adaptive Devices Designed for St. Mary's Kids." St. Mary's Healthcare System for Children, January 15, 2018. http://www.stmaryskids.org/news /lynbrook-high-school-students-present-3d-printed -adaptive-devices-designed-for-st-marys-kids.

MSWguide.org. "What Is Medical Social Work?" January 14, 2018. http://www.mswguide.org/careers/medical -social-work.

National Parks Service. "Theodore Roosevelt and Conservation." November 17, 2017. http://www.nps .gov/thro/learn/historyculture/theodore-roosevelt-and -conservation.htm.

Public Broadcasting Service (PBS. "The Modern Environmental Movement." *American Experience*, January 5, 2018. http://www.pbs.org/wgbh /americanexperience/features/earth -days-modern-environmental-movement.

O'Brien, Patrick, and Susan Davis-Ali. "5 Do's and Don'ts for Building a Winning Resume." *USA Today*, September 27, 2013. http://www.usatoday.com /story/news/nation/2013/09/26/5-tips-for-a-great -resume/2875465.

Pardes, Arielle. "10 Things Social Workers Want You to Know About What They Really Do." *Cosmopolitan*, October 5, 2017. http://www.cosmopolitan.com/career /a59947/things-i-wish-i-knew-social-worker-career.

Peled, Shachar. "At 7, This Boy Runs a Company and Saves for College." CNN, January 15, 2018. http:// www.cnn.com/2017/03/09/us/recycling-boy-trnd/index .html.

Ryan, Liz. "How To Answer Ten Common Interview Questions—with Confidence." *Forbes*, December 11, 2017. http://www.forbes.com/sites/lizryan/2017/12/09 /how-to-answer-ten-common-interview-questions-with -confidence/#724c2e043ef1.

Smith, Emily. Email interview with the author, February 13, 2018.

Teaching.org. "An Interview with Program Coordinator, Becky Adair—Teaching.org—Directory of Teaching Schools and List of Teaching Degree Programs." January 18, 2018. http://teaching.org/resources /an-interview-with-program-coordinator-becky-adair.

2U.com. "What Is Social Work?" January 2, 2018. http:// socialworklicensemap.com/become-a-social-worker /what-is-social-work.

Index

About the Author

Jessica Shaw has a BA in psychology from Texas State University. She has worked in human services and taught preschool and currently writes nonfiction, fiction, and poetry for children and young adults, including standardized testing material and work appearing in numerous children's publications.

Photo Credits

Cover Tom Merton/Caiaimage/Getty Images; cover and interior pages (map) © iStockphoto.com/Pingebat; p. 3, interior pages border (bull) quietbits/Shutterstock.com; p. 5 Agence France Presse/AFP/Getty Images; p. 9 wavebreakmedia/Shutterstock.com; p. 11 Robert Sabo /NY Daily News/Getty Images; p. 16 The Washington Post /Getty Images; pp. 19, 22, 29 © AP Images; p. 25 monkeybusinessimages/iStock/Thinkstock; p. 27 Wavebreak Media/Thinkstock; p. 31 Jo Ann Snover /Shutterstock.com; pp. 34–35 Eliot Elisofon/The LIFE Picture Collection/Getty Images; p. 39 Felineus /Shutterstock.com; p. 42 Library of Congress Prints and Photographs; p. 45 Rawpixel.com/Shutterstock.com; pp. 46–47 Kathryn Scott Osler/The Denver Post /Getty Images; pp. 50–51 Anne Cusack/Los Angeles Times /Getty Images; p. 52 Kathy Hutchins/Shutterstock.com; p. 55 MindStorm/Shutterstock.com; p. 58 Natee Meepian /Shutterstock.com; p. 60 Stephen Coburn /Shutterstock.com; p. 64 Win McNamee/Getty Images.

Design and Layout: Nicole Russo-Duca; Editor: Bethany Bryan; Photo Researcher: Nicole DiMella